This book belongs to...

.... Haneef ....

LONDON, NEW YORK,
MELBOURNE, MUNICH, AND DELHI

Writer Angela Royston
Art Editor Nigel Hazle
Photographer Barrie Watts

REVISED PAPERBACK EDITION
Project Editor Charlie Gardner
Designer David Meier
Production Controller Vivianne Ridgeway

First published in the Great Britain in 1991

This revised edition published in 2007 by
Dorling Kindersley Limited
80 Strand, London, WC2R 0RL

07 08 09 10 11 10 9 8 7 6 5 4 3 2 1
SD331 – 08/07

A CIP catalogue record for this book is
available from the British Library

ISBN: 978-1-4053-2730-5

Printed and bound in China by Hung Hing

Discover more at
www.dk.com

See how they grow

Duck

In the nest

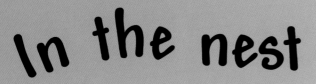

Inside this egg a new duckling is growing. It is me! I am just beginning to hatch.

My mother has laid her eggs in this nest.
She sits on them to keep them warm.

Just hatched

I have chipped away my shell and now I'm pushing myself out.

Whew! Finally, I'm out of my egg.

I can see, hear, stand, and walk.
I can cheep, too.
But where is my mother?

First swim

I am two days old now. I am going to the pond for my first swim.

As soon as I am in the water, I start to swim.

I use my webbed feet to push
me through the water.

Feeding

I am seven days old and
getting bigger.
I like to explore new things.

This bowl has water in it.
I search with my beak for
things to eat.

Now I've jumped right into the bowl!

In the water

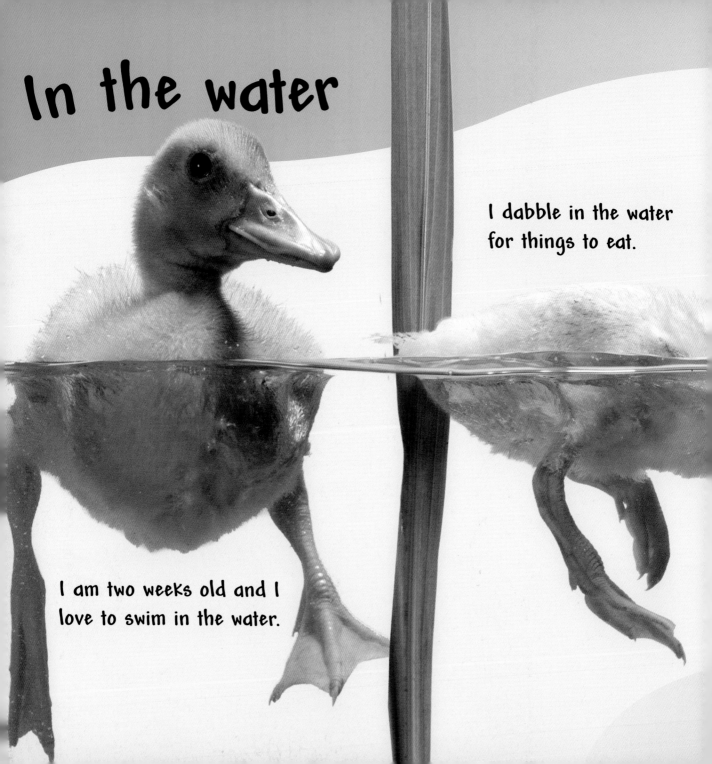

I dabble in the water for things to eat.

I am two weeks old and I love to swim in the water.

I shake the water off my feathers.

New feathers

I am three weeks old. My
yellow down is falling out
and new white feathers
are beginning
to grow.

I stay close to the other
ducklings. Our mother
watches for danger.

Sometimes we huddle together. Our fuzzy feathers help keep us warm.

Almost grown up

I am six weeks old and
nearly grown up.

All my feathers are white and my
wings are bigger and stronger.

See how much I have grown. This bowl is small now, but it seemed big when I first jumped into it!

See how I grew

The egg

One hour old

Two days old

Seven days old

Two weeks old

Three weeks old

Six weeks old

See how I grow

See how they grow

Duck
Watch a tiny yellow duckling become a beautiful white duck
ISBN 978-1-4053-2730-5

Kitten
See a tiny kitten become a playful young cat
ISBN 978-1-4053-2727-5

Puppy
Watch a playful puppy grow into a mature dog
ISBN 978-1-4053-2726-8

Rabbit
See a tiny pink baby grow into a bouncy white rabbit
ISBN 978-1-4053-2731-2